One-Minute
INSIGHTS
for MEN

JIM GEORGE

HARVEST HOUSE PUBLISHERS
EUGENE, OREGON

Cover by Harvest House Publishers, Inc., Eugene, Oregon

Cover photo © iStockphoto / sharply_done

Devotions taken from *A Man After God's Own Heart Devotional*

ONE-MINUTE INSIGHTS FOR MEN
Copyright © 2013 by Jim George
Published by Harvest House Publishers
Eugene, Oregon 97402
www.harvesthousepublishers.com

ISBN 978-0-7369-5742-7 (pbk.)

ISBN 978-0-7369-5744-1 (eBook)

Printed in the United States of America

17 18 19 20 21 / BP-NI / 10 9 8 7 6 5

A Note
from Jim

It is my prayer that this practical book of exhortations and inspirational thoughts will help you remember that God is not looking for perfection. All He asks for is a man who is progressing in his desire to become a man after God's own heart.

Jim George

Waiting for God's Answers

When you think your prayers aren't being answered, you tend to get discouraged and cry out, "God, why aren't You helping me?"

Yet God has promised to answer your prayers: "Ask, and it will be given to you; seek, and you will find; knock, and it will be opened to you" (Matthew 7:7). However, sometimes you don't see the answer for a while, or God may say no because He has a different—and better—plan.

So you are exhorted to ask. But your request must be…

- in faith (Matthew 21:22),
- without selfish motives (James 4:3), and
- according to the will of God (1 John 5:14-15).

Lord, I confess that I'm not good at waiting for Your answers to my prayers. But as I wait, I believe You will build my faith, purify my heart, and show me Your will. Thank You!

Always Ready to Listen

When you fail to pray, you end up feeling distant from God. And that, in turn, makes you even more reluctant to pray.

No matter how distant you might feel from the Lord, God is always close by. He hasn't changed, moved, disappeared, or lost interest in you. So close the gap. Take a simple step toward God and talk to Him. The more you do this, the more comfortable you'll become communicating with Him. And the more you pray, the more opportunity you'll have to ask for His help for yourself and on behalf of others. And the more you ask, the more answers and guidance you'll receive. No matter what your situation, God is always ready to listen!

Father, thank You for always being near, always listening, and always caring. Help me to look to You in every situation and to never allow a gap to develop between us. Amen.

Too Busy
to Pray?

Often when you fail to pray, you say it's because you're so busy. But in reality, it's not your schedule that keeps you from praying. It's your failure to realize the importance of prayer and *make* the time to pray.

And instead of relying upon the power of prayer in all that you do, you turn to your feeble wisdom and energy. You roll up your sleeves and get busy, turning to your own power instead of God's.

If your life is so busy you can't pray, have you ever considered it's because you haven't taken time to ask God for help with your priorities? Turn to Him, and He will give you the discernment that enables you to use your time well so that you are able to pray.

God, show me—what have I prioritized above
my time with You? What have I depended on
instead of You? Help me assess my priorities
today and keep prayer at the top of the list. Amen.

When You
Need Wisdom

Are you experiencing a difficult problem in your life right now? Are you at a crossroad with regard to a major decision? Are you struggling with issues you don't have answers for? If yes, hear this promise from your heavenly Father: "If any of you lacks wisdom, let him ask of God, who gives to all liberally and without reproach, and it will be given to him" (James 1:5).

God stands ready to give you wisdom. Remember, He is the source of it: "Oh, the depth of the riches both of the wisdom and knowledge of God!" (Romans 11:33). And when you don't understand what is happening, you need to wait, trust Him, and rest in His care. He is always faithful to His own.

Lord, I'll be the first to admit it—I need Your wisdom! Help me to wait on You and to put into practice the things You show me in Your Word. Amen.

Saying Yes to God

God is able to use a man who is willing to do whatever He says. By this I mean a person who listens to and obeys Him.

We see confirmation of this in the Bible. For example, the apostle Paul was asked to *get up*—and spread the gospel. Abraham was asked to *give up*—to sacrifice his son Isaac up to God, until God spared Isaac. Moses was asked to *speak up*—to confront Pharaoh about letting the people of Israel go. And Daniel was asked to *stand up*—to not yield to demands to compromise his faith. In every case, God rewarded the obedience these men showed.

When you yield yourself in complete and wholehearted obedience to God, He can do great things through you.

> *Father, show me how I can honor You in everything I do at home, at work, and when I'm just having fun. I choose in advance to say yes to You in all I do! Amen.*

The Power of Obedience

When you consider the extraordinary ways God worked through men such as Moses and Paul, you may think, *I can't measure up to people like them. I don't have what they had.*

But you must realize that these "heroes" of the faith were just common, ordinary people. It was their obedience—their complete yieldedness to God—that gave them uncommon strength and faith. They submitted their lives to God, which freed God to work through them.

I don't know about you, but their examples inspire me to re-evaluate my own obedience. Am I reluctant to listen to God because I think He is asking the impossible? Am I failing to make myself available to Him because I'm doubtful or afraid? Your part is to simply obey, and God will do His part.

God, I see now that You can do anything through me if I will simply yield myself to You. Help me to make myself more available to You today. Amen.

At the Center
of God's Will

Do you know what I believe is the icing on the cake of obedience, what I believe to be one of the most compelling reasons for choosing to obey God? It is this: Obedience leads to a powerful, confident life. When you are obedient, and when you allow yourself to be led by God through the unexpected, you then have a confidence based on the fact that you know you are exactly where God wants you to be. You won't find yourself doubting the circumstances in your life or the direction things are going. We'll have the inner peace and joy that comes from knowing you are at the center of God's will!

Lord, thank You for leading me to the center of Your will. Help me to see Your hand in everything that comes my way as I follow You today. Amen.

God-confidence

Are you fearful because God appears to be moving you in an unexpected direction? Is the unknown causing you to waver on the path of obedience? Take heart in your resolve. Walk in confidence with God. Walk as King David did, declaring, "Though I walk through the valley of the shadow of death, I will fear no evil; for You are with me" (Psalm 23:4).

Though you might not know where God's will is taking you, you can trust God to watch over and stay with you. Though life may take surprising turns, they are not unexpected to God. He knows what is happening and why, and all He calls you to do is to trust Him.

Father, I affirm that as long as You lead me and I walk with You, I have nothing to fear. I resolve to follow You today, knowing that I'm never safer than when I'm with You. Amen.

Making the Best Decisions

What if you're uncertain about an important decision you must make? How can you seek God's input? Here are the four C's you'll find helpful for the times when you need guidance:

Commands from the inspired Word of God

Competent and wise counselors

Circumstances and changing conditions

Conscience aided by the Holy Spirit

God can use any or all of these means to give direction to you if you are ready to listen. It may take time, but that's okay. Making use of these resources will help you to make informed choices that honor and glorify God.

God, I want to make wise decisions that glorify You. Help me to keep my eyes and ears open so I can learn from You and honor You in all I say and do. Amen.

Great Is
His Faithfulness

How often do you take time to pause and revel in how faithful God has been to you?

Recognizing God's good help to you is important. It's when you remember His unceasing care that you are reminded He will carry you through every situation in life, no matter how bad. It was God's faithfulness in adversity that led King David to write, "I waited patiently for the Lord; and He inclined to me, and heard my cry. He also brought me up out of a horrible pit, out of the miry clay; and set my feet upon a rock, and established my steps. He has put a new song in my mouth—praise to our God; many will see it and fear, and will trust in the Lord" (Psalm 40:1-3).

Lord, You've pulled me out of a few "horrible pits" and established my steps. Help me to never forget what You have done, to always praise You, and to eagerly share Your faithfulness with others. Amen.

When It's Hard to Have Hope

When something terrible happens in your life, are you ever tempted to ask, "What good could come out of this?" It *looks* like a disaster. It *feels* like a disaster. Therefore you conclude, "It *is* a disaster!"

That's when you want to remember God's promise, "I know the thoughts that I think toward you... thoughts of peace and not of evil, to give you a future and a hope" (Jeremiah 29:11). And then there's Romans 8:28, which says, "All things work together for good to those who love God."

God doesn't tell you you'll escape suffering or pain. Rather, He promises to miraculously use even bad situations for your ultimate good, and He assures you that you have a great future ahead of you. Let these promises sustain you when you find it's hard to have hope.

Father, when I suffer, please strengthen me with Your Word and Your Spirit so I can endure with joy, knowing that You ultimately have great things in store for me. Amen.

Always There
with You

Do you ever think about the fact that God knows, in advance, everything that will happen?

That means there is nothing that takes God by surprise—even the difficult crises in your life. So when you find yourself worried about tomorrow, lift your cares up to the Lord. He has already seen the future, and because He is faithful, He will give you whatever you need to persevere through your problems. In the same way that He sustained the psalmist "through the valley of the shadow of death" (Psalm 23:4), He will preserve and comfort you in every trial you face. That's why you can rejoice with David and say, "Surely goodness and mercy shall follow me all the days of my life" (verse 6).

> God, I don't know what might happen tomorrow, but You do. I can't cause good to come from any crisis, but You can. I won't always be able to meet my own needs, but You will. Thank You.

Restoring
Hope

When worry strikes, we usually get discouraged or even depressed. We respond to life negatively, and take our eyes off God and His promises to take care of us. The next time worry strikes, here's how you can restore your hope:

Pray—"Be anxious for nothing, but in everything by prayer and supplication…let your requests be made known to God" (Philippians 3:6).

Trust—Refuse to worry about circumstances beyond your control. Remember, they are still in God's control (Psalm 135:6).

Give thanks—"In everything give thanks" (1 Thessalonians 5:18). When you thank God even for the hard things in life, you are saying, "Lord, I am confident You will use this for my good."

> *Lord, it's so easy for me to focus on the negative. Help me redeem my worried thoughts by using them as reminders to pray, to express my trust in You, and to give thanks. Amen.*

One Decision
at a Time

How did men like Abraham, Daniel, and Paul become men who accomplished great things for God? There wasn't any secret formula to success for them. In fact, they were ordinary men like you and me. What made them effective leaders was their willingness to obey God, one decision at a time.

Your impact on the lives of others—your family, the people at your church, your workmates—is cultivated with each decision you make, no matter how small. It's the little things—such as reading your Bible, praying, going to church, and standing up for your faith—that add influence to your life. The key to a powerful Christian life is to obey God one decision at a time. Then He will trust you with more.

Father, may this day be filled with small steps of obedience. I pray that each choice I make today—large or small—will help me influence others for good. Amen.

Letting God Lead

When you submit yourself to God and obey Him, you allow Him to do what He desires in your life. You make it possible for Him to lead you wherever He wants to use you.

At the same time, you'll experience the confidence that comes from knowing you are exactly where God wants you to be. You'll experience the joy of knowing you are at the center of God's will. Then you, along with Paul, can confidently lead and boldly influence others as you declare, "Imitate me, just as I also imitate Christ" (1 Corinthians 11:1).

That's why obeying God is so important. It allows Him to work through you, and it gives you a secure confidence for everyday living. Isn't that what you long for?

God, when I'm intimidated by a huge task before me, help me to focus on simply obeying You one step at a time. And may my life encourage others to do the same. Amen.

Attending to His Word

If you struggle with obeying God, ask Him to give you the strength to obey His commands. And that strength will come as you...

- faithfully read His Word,
- faithfully hear the preaching of His Word,
- faithfully listen to wise counsel from His Word, and
- faithfully deal with sin in your life as revealed by the piercing light of His Word.

Can you see how God's Word is such an important part of your life? Your willingness to obey the Lord is a key step toward experiencing God's blessings, and it will enable you to become a man God can use to make a difference.

Lord, thank You for pouring Your strength into me as I attend to Your Word. May every blessing and every trial in my life turn my obedient attention to Your Word. Amen.

Rising to
the Occasion

The path of obedience is seldom easy. It certainly wasn't easy for the Christians in the New Testament era. When they preached the gospel in Jerusalem, the Jewish religious leaders told them to stop. How did they respond? They courageously declared, "Whether it is right in the sight of God to listen to you more than to God, you judge. For we cannot but speak the things which we have seen and heard" (Acts 4:19-20).

And what was the effect of their obedience? "They were all filled with the Holy Spirit, and they spoke the word of God with boldness" (verse 31). As a result, people came to Christ, and the church grew—all because they were willing to overcome challenges in their pursuit of obeying God. Are you ready to rise to the occasion?

Father, help me recognize the steps of obedience You ask me to make today. And when my commitment is challenged, help me rise to the occasion and glorify You in all I do. Amen.

Keeping Your Eye on the Prize

Because obedience has its challenges, it's the less-traveled path. Disobedience, on the other hand, is the more well-worn way. In fact, it is characterized by gridlock! Why? Because it's the easy way out. It's the road we're tempted to take when things get sticky or uncomfortable. It's the path of least resistance, and sadly, it's the path that makes us men of little or no positive impact.

As you run the race for Christ, you'll face hurdles that trip you up, knock you down, or pressure you to compromise God's standards. That's why Paul urges you to "press toward the goal for the prize of the upward call of God in Jesus Christ" (Philippians 3:14). If you keep your eye on the prize at the finish line, you'll have what it takes to overcome life's challenges.

God, instead of sneaking around the hurdles of life on the path of least resistance, I want to sail over those challenges on the high road of obedience. Please help me. Amen.

Victory over the Flesh

Every Christian man battles with the flesh—even the great apostle Paul struggled (see Romans 7:21-24). How can you M-A-S-T-E-R this challenge?

Monitor your time with those who drag you down.

Account for your struggles to a more mature believer.

Strengthen your inner man through the Bible and prayer.

Train your eyes to avoid things that stir fleshly desires.

Exercise purity in relationships with the opposite sex.

Run from the lusts of the flesh.

Victory *is* possible. Make these steps a regular part of your life!

Lord, thank You for reminding me that I am not a helpless victim. Empower me to master my fleshly desires, I pray, as I put these tools into practice. Amen.

All Ear

Have you ever tried to define *obedience*? That's the challenge a missionary ran up against as he was translating the Bible into a foreign language. Taking a break from his search for a meaning, he called to his dog. When the dog came running, a tribal observer said, "Your dog was all ear." Instantly the missionary had the words he needed to define *obedience*—"to be all ear."

How about you? Are you "all ear" when it comes to hearing what God says in His Word?

Ask the Lord to help you respond with eagerness to Scripture. You'll find this easier to do when you follow the example set by King David: "Your word I have hidden in my heart, that I might not sin against you" (Psalm 119:11).

Father, as I hide Your Word in my heart, help me to listen to its promptings and hear its life-giving message. And then, give me strength to obey—to be all ear. Amen.

Enduring Opposition

Anytime you stand up for what you believe, you will experience opposition—you can count on it! As Paul told his young disciple, Timothy, "*All* who desire to live godly in Christ Jesus will suffer persecution" (2 Timothy 3:12).

Earlier in 2 Timothy, Paul wrote, "You...must endure hardship as a good soldier of Jesus Christ. No one engaged in warfare entangles himself with the affairs of this life" (2:3-4). You are called to live boldly by different standards—God's standards.

Yes, it will be difficult. But such hardship is nothing compared to what you'll gain—God's blessing for your obedience and a clear conscience for doing what is right.

> *God, how are You asking me to stand up for what I believe today? When opposition comes my way, give me strength to bear it with grace and maintain a clear conscience. Amen.*

Tapping into God's Strength

The beauty of obedience is that what God *expects* you to do, He also *enables* you to do. The strength comes from Him. You just need a willing heart.

The apostle Paul wrote, "Be strong in the Lord and in the power of His might" (Ephesians 6:10). God has made this strength available to you, and it's pretty remarkable. Paul spoke of "the *exceeding greatness* of His power toward us who believe, according to the working of His mighty power" (Ephesians 1:19).

The power of God triumphs over all else. And you have access to it. How? Through full dependence upon Him, "praying always with all prayer and supplication in the Spirit" (6:18).

> *Lord, this is amazing. When I say yes to You—and mean it—You will give me the strength to follow through. Thank You for the "exceeding greatness" of Your power in me! Amen.*

Rejoicing in Every Victory

Growing in obedience to God is a lifelong process. It will never end. So you can expect to struggle against the desires of the flesh time and time again.

That's why it's so important to remember that spiritual growth happens one step at a time, one victory at a time. It may not seem like it at the moment, but every one of your victories—even the small ones—add up and have a cumulative effect, bringing you toward greater spiritual maturity.

So rejoice in even the smallest victories. Thank God for every time He enables you to make a right choice. And you'll find yourself inspired to persevere as new challenges come your way.

Father, help me to see the importance of every tiny step of obedience I take today. Thank You for using those steps to make me stronger, more mature, and more like You. Amen.

The Key
to Focus

Have you ever felt like your life is scattered, as if you're going ten different directions? Have you wished your life was more focused?

If there's one lesson we can learn from the apostle Paul, it's the value of discipline. All his energies were passionately channeled in one direction—toward winning a "crown that will last forever" (1 Corinthians 9:25 NIV). Whereas many people chase after earthly prizes, or crowns that won't last, Paul pursued an eternal prize. He wanted to know Christ, the power of His resurrection, and the fellowship of His sufferings (Philippians 3:10). And he counted everything else but loss (3:3-7).

What is motivating you? Is Christ truly first in your life? When He is, you'll have focus.

> *God, I want to be passionate, focused, and directed. Alert me today if I start going several directions at once. Bring all my responsibilities together into a unified life of following You. Amen.*

Profitable for All Things

We live in a health-conscious society. Diet plans and exercise regiments abound, and we're reminded again and again of the benefits of eating right and good physical training.

Even the Bible acknowledges this, saying that bodily exercise "profits" us (1 Timothy 4:8). Yet notice what it says next: "But godliness is profitable for all things, having promise of the life that now is and of that which is to come." So while physical training has some value, spiritual training has a lot more. In fact, it's "profitable for *all* things." That includes your marriage, your children, your job, your ministry, and even your life in eternity!

How are you doing in your growth toward godliness—that is, becoming more like God as much as is humanly possible?

> *Lord, help me assess my spiritual training regimen and make adjustments where necessary. Thank You for the promise that my growth in godliness is not only possible but also profitable! Amen.*

The Rewards of Discipline

I'm sure you've heard the slogan "No pain, no gain." Usually we see those words posted in a gym or over a locker-room door. But these same four words are also a perfect paraphrase of the personal philosophy of the apostle Paul, who said, "I strike a blow to my body and make it my slave so that…I myself will not be disqualified for the prize" (1 Corinthians 9:27 NIV).

This kind of discipline requires effort and sacrifice. But it's well worthwhile, for you'll receive a double prize—the eternal prize Paul is talking about, and the earthly prize of accomplishment and impact. Indeed, personal discipline brings great rewards.

Father, as I focus on the prize right now, the effort, sacrifice, and pain of discipline seem much more manageable. Help me to focus on the prize all through the day today. Amen.

Imitating God

Are you a spiritually sensitive man? By way of definition, this means walking through life with a God-consciousness. It means knowing how God would act, talk, and respond to life's situations.

How can you develop this kind of sensitivity? A key way is to observe God in action in the Bible. For example, as you see how He responded graciously to His fallen creation and sacrificed His only Son for us, you begin to understand how you should be more loving, giving, and selfless. As you see His other traits—His patience, His wisdom, His goodness— you'll discover character qualities you'll want to imitate in your own life.

So observe God carefully. Learn from His example. And you'll grow in spiritual sensitivity.

> *God, how can I imitate You at work today? At home? In the community? Show me how my simple words and actions can reflect Your saving work in the world. Amen.*

Mastering
God's Word

When I was young in the Christian faith, a man came to our church to teach a seminar. It was evident that he knew his Bible very well. I admired his grasp of Scripture, and wished I had the same.

After the seminar, I summoned the courage to ask how he came to know the Bible so well. I expected him to say it was his theological training, or his ability to interpret Scripture. But to my surprise, he said it was a lifetime of just reading the Bible regularly, day in and day out.

That's pretty simple, isn't it? What a joy it was to realize every believer could have the same kind of knowledge. All it takes is faithful and consistent reading.

> *Lord, I pray that You would open my eyes as I read the Scriptures. May my heart be like good soil so the seed of Your Word will go deep and produce a good crop. Amen.*

Godly Ambition

Ambition can be both positive and negative. An example of the latter is people who have scratched their way to the top and, in the process, left their claw marks on the backs of you and others whom they climbed over in order to reach their goal.

That's not the kind of ambition we as Christian men should have. No, we are to have a godly ambition—that is, a desire to serve the Lord and focus on fulfilling His will. God's kind of man strives solely for the glory of God and the good of others. I believe this is part of what Paul had in mind when he said, "Imitate me, just as I also imitate Christ" (1 Corinthians 11:1). Let's follow Paul's example by bringing our ambition in line with God's will.

God, when I am consumed by selfish ambition, help me focus on glorifying You and serving others. And when I lack ambition, remind me of the tremendous prize of knowing You. Amen.

The Value
of Goals

What are your goals in life? Have you defined them yet? Goals can help you in a lot of ways. For example, goals give *definition*—they take daydreams and make them concrete. Goals give *focus*—they help you know how to spend your time, and set aside time-wasters. Goals give *motivation*—they give you something to aim for, they help prod you onward when the going gets rough. Goals help you with *decision-making*—they equip you to make the best decisions about how to spend your time, money, and energy. And goals help you to have an *impact*—when you achieve them, you'll have grown as a person and hopefully others will benefit from your efforts.

So set some goals…and become the kind of man who makes a difference!

> *Lord, guide me as I assess my goals today. Help me set constructive goals, prioritize them appropriately, and submit them to Your leadership. May my goals lead to my highest goal of knowing You. Amen.*

Using Time Well

The sooner we realize that life is but a vapor (James 4:14), the more likely we are to make sure we are using our time well.

That doesn't mean you can't take time to have fun and relax. Rather, it means making sure you have your priorities in order. At the top of the list is your spiritual health. That's because it affects everything else you do. When things are right between you and God and you're spending time in His Word, that will help you align the rest of your priorities properly, which include caring for your family, managing your finances wisely, maintaining good physical health, giving your best on the job, and serving others in your church. When you've taken care of these priorities, you can be confident you are using your time well.

Father, do my priorities bring glory to You? Do they help me make the most of my short time on this earth? Help me re-evaluate my priorities and make any necessary adjustments. Amen.

A Healthy Perspective

God cares about your body and health. Scripture says that…

- your body is a *stewardship* from God
  (1 Corinthians 6:19-20)
- your body is the *temple* of the Holy Spirit
  (1 Corinthians 3:16)
- your body is meant to *glorify* God
  (1 Corinthians 6:19-20)

So how are you doing? Many people these days could eat better and use more exercise. Are you among them? Do you view your body as something that God has entrusted into your care? Having that perspective may help you to be more diligent about your physical health. And that, in turn, will help you to enjoy life more and live longer.

God, thank You for showing me this strong connection between my physical and spiritual health. How can I be a good steward of my body and glorify You with it? Lead me, Lord. Amen.

The Gift
of Friends

Friends are a gift from the Lord. You should cultivate friendships with other men, especially other Christian men who will encourage you in your faith and give good advice. The Bible says, "As iron sharpens iron, so a man sharpens the countenance of his friend" (Proverbs 27:17).

Are you friends with men who are a positive influence on your life, who encourage and build you up in the faith? And are you making the effort to grow spiritually so you, in turn, can be that kind of friend to others?

If you are in need of such friends, ask God to lead you to the right people. And be willing to take time to be a friend to other men who would benefit from your wisdom and experience.

> *Lord, help me to build replenishing friendships with other men. Whom can I look to as an example? Whom can I encourage? Thank You for my friends! Amen.*

Little Choices,
Big Decisions

There are a myriad of thoughts penned on the importance of choices. You've probably heard this one:

Little choices determine habit;
Habit carves and molds character,
Which makes the big decisions.

What does that tell you? Even the little things count. If ever you're tempted to cut corners and do things the easy way, or do your work halfheartedly because others aren't watching, eventually your little choices are going to become habits that affect the bigger decisions you make in life. This is especially true with regard to sin. Taking it lightly can lead to poor decision-making down the road. So consider every choice carefully, no matter how small, for it will affect the bigger decisions you make.

God, help me to pay attention to my activities today and to consider the importance of the small choices I will make. May each one be a reflection of my one big choice to follow You. Amen.

Understanding Temptation

When it comes to *temptation* and *sin*, there's an important distinction to make: Temptation is not sin. When you are tempted, you are faced with a choice. You still have the opportunity to resist and not fall into sin. But when you succumb, then you've gone from temptation to sin.

So if you find yourself struggling with temptation, you haven't done anything wrong yet. Just make sure you look to God for help, for He has promised, "No temptation has overtaken you except such as is common to man; but God is faithful, who will not allow you to be tempted beyond what you are able, but with the temptation will also make the way of escape, that you may be able to bear it" (1 Corinthians 10:13).

> *Lord, thank You for the promise that You will help me to bear every temptation that comes my way today. When I am tempted, help me remember to run to You. Amen.*

Winning
the Battle

When it comes to temptation, you are not alone. The Bible says this struggle is "common to man" (1 Corinthians 10:13). That means we all battle with temptation and sin. And thankfully, God has given you the resources you need for victory:

a new law (life in Christ),
a guide (the Holy Spirit),
a guidebook (the Bible),
and guides (wise counselors).

So you are fully equipped to withstand the temptations you face each day. Statements of "I can't" no longer apply to us. In Jesus Christ, it's "I can!" As Paul said, "I *can* do all things through Christ who strengthens me" (Philippians 4:13).

> *God, I affirm that You have given me everything I need to win the battle over temptation. When I am tempted, please help me remember to say, "In Christ, I can defeat this!" Amen.*

Protecting Yourself

God promised that when it comes to temptation, He has provided "the way of escape" (1 Corinthians 10:13). But even before you get to the point you are tempted, there are measures you can take to protect yourself from falling into sin.

First, you have God's Word, which helps you to discern right from wrong. Reading, listening to, and obeying it will help you resist sin. *Second*, you can avoid places and situations where you might experience temptation. *Third*, you can avoid getting involved with people who might pressure you to participate in sin. And fourth, avoid allowing your eyes to roam. Job "made a covenant with [his] eyes not to look lustfully at a young woman" (Job 31:1 NIV).

Providing temptation with fewer opportunities to strike is a great way to protect and preserve yourself.

> *Heavenly Father, lead me not into temptation today. And help me make smart choices about where I go, what I fill my mind with, and whom I spend my time with. Amen.*

Your Weapon
Against Temptation

Have you ever noticed how Jesus handled temptation?

When Satan tempted the Lord during His 40 days in the wilderness, Jesus responded to every temptation by saying, "It is written…It is written…It is written" (Matthew 4:4-10). Why? Because God's Word is truth, and only truth can refute the lies Satan sends our way when he tempts us. Satan wants us to believe sin will give us pleasure and satisfaction. By contrast, God's truth warns that sin leads to guilt and emptiness.

Are you well-armed with God's Word? Do you know what it says? Are you fighting your battles against temptation with the sword of the Spirit, the Word of God (Ephesians 6:17)? Get to know what the Bible says about the kinds of temptations you face.

> *Lord, help me to identify the lies that are likely to bombard me today. Thank You for arming me with the truth and teaching me to use the sword of the Spirit effectively. Amen.*

Leading by Serving

I'm sure you agree that Jesus Christ was the most influential man who ever lived. No one has or ever will match the impact He had.

What makes Him all the more remarkable is He wasn't an autocrat, a leader running roughshod over people or demanding respect and obedience. Rather, He was a humble servant. He "did not come to be served, but to serve, and to give His life" (Mark 10:45). After He performed the lowly task of washing the disciples' feet, He said, "I have given you an example, that you should do as I have done to you" (John 13:15).

Whose feet could you wash today? What opportunities do you have right now to serve rather than be served?

> *Jesus, You are the King of kings and Lord of lords, yet You chose to live as a humble servant. May I follow in Your steps today as You give me opportunities to serve those around me. Amen.*

It Really Does Matter

Sometimes we do an act of service and then get the feeling that it wasn't a valuable enough contribution to the church, or that nobody noticed or cared. Therefore we feel like what we did was a failure. It didn't really matter.

But no service that is done for God is a failure. Though from a human standpoint your labors might be overlooked or underappreciated, from a divine standpoint, that's never the case. God knows everything you do, and He will bless and reward you accordingly.

While recognition and thank-yous are nice to receive, they're not the reason you serve the Lord. You serve to please and honor Him. And the joy that comes from serving Him well will satisfy you more than any human applause could.

Father, thank You for seeing everything—even what is done in secret. As I find opportunities to serve others today, help me to remember that my reward comes from You. Amen.

Energized
by Love

There is no greater example of loving service than that seen in a mother. It's remarkable the great sacrifice a mom makes for her children when they're feeling sick or they're struggling with something in their life.

Did you know the apostle Paul served with that kind of love? In his letter to the Christians in Thessalonica, he wrote, "We were gentle among you, just as a nursing mother cherishes her own children...we were well pleased to impart to you...our own lives, because you had become dear to us" (1 Thessalonians 2:7-8).

Is your service energized by love as well? Do you show love to those whom you serve?

> *Lord, I confess that my love is often shallow and weak. Please pour Your love into me and through me to touch everyone I meet today, especially those who feel rejected and alone. Amen.*

What Service Communicates

Do you realize that even if you say nothing to the people you serve, you are still teaching volumes? You nurture others by your Christlike example of selfless service. What wife wouldn't be built up and encouraged by a husband who loved her by helping make her job as a wife and mother easier? What child wouldn't be motivated and inspired to follow Christ after having seen the Lord's love demonstrated by his or her own father? What co-worker wouldn't see that there's something different about a Christian when you serve wholeheartedly without complaint?

Your nurturing service to others at home, at church, or on the job—providing help, encouragement, and hope—will point unbelievers toward God and edify believers in their faith.

Father, may my humble service to others today shout out the tremendously good news that You are reconciling us to Yourself and restoring us according to Your original design. Amen.

For the Good of Others

By definition, serving others means being willing to make sacrifices for their good. A supreme example of this is the Good Samaritan in Luke 10:30-37. He sacrificed time by stopping to help the wounded traveler. He sacrificed his possessions by bandaging and dressing the man's wounds. He sacrificed his personal transportation by carrying the man to an inn. He sacrificed his life by taking care of the man personally. And he sacrificed his money by giving a day's wages and in essence a blank check to an innkeeper for the continued care of the wounded man.

Do you think the Good Samaritan had a positive impact? Without a doubt! When you serve, then, don't focus on what you've given up, but on what others have gained.

God, all I have is Yours. Help me to joyfully sacrifice my time and possessions for others today, mindful that You will supply all I need according to Your riches in glory in Christ Jesus. Amen.

A Heart
for Service

If your desire is for God to use you more as a servant, the most important first step you can take is to make sure you're serving those who live under your roof—your wife and children. What you are at home is what you are!

Then look at your major life commitments, such as your job. There, you'll find many opportunities to show Christlike love, sacrifice, and patience toward others. And if you belong to a club or sports team, showing a servant's heart in everything you do will cause people to see God and Christianity in a positive light.

The more you manifest a servant's heart in all you do, the more of an impact you'll have on people's lives.

Lord, open my eyes today so I can see opportunities to serve my family, my co-workers, and my friends. Help me to serve with joy as You strengthen me through Your Word and Spirit. Amen.

Giving
Your All

When you serve, sometimes you can fall into the mind-set that because you're doing it for free, or because people should be grateful for your sacrifice, it's okay if you do less than your very best. You may rationalize that it's okay to cut corners.

But a good servant gives his all. For example, the apostle Paul told the Christian leaders in Ephesus, "Remember that for three years I did not cease to warn everyone night and day with tears" (Acts 20:31). He sacrificed himself without ceasing—and to the point of tears!

Do you view your opportunities to serve as a stewardship from God? When you do, you'll find yourself motivated to serve with excellence.

Father, help me to serve with excellence today, mindful that my service to others is pleasing to You. Thank You for Paul's inspiring example— may I follow in his steps. Amen.

When the Going Gets Tough

A servant of God is willing to endure pain, suffering, and persecution in order to accomplish God's work. Remember the apostle Paul? He faced tremendous adversity—prisons, beatings, and even shipwreck. Yet his ministry bore much fruit—all because he was willing to keep going.

How firm are you in your commitment to serve? Do you give up easily at the least sign of resistance? Or are you willing to withstand the opposition that often arises in the course of serving the Lord?

When you find yourself getting discouraged, remember the examples of Paul and Jesus. They paid a great price, yet realized even greater gains. Hang in there, for what you do will reap eternal rewards.

God, thank You for strengthening me with all power according to Your glorious might so that I may have great endurance and patience. Because You are committed to me, I can be committed to You. Amen.

A Life
Without Regrets

Paul saw his life as a sacrificial offering to God. He wrote, "I am already being poured out as a drink offering, and the time of my departure is at hand. I have fought the good fight, I have finished the race, I have kept the faith" (2 Timothy 4:6-7).

Because Paul had given his all, he could say he was ready to leave earth. He didn't have any regrets haunting him. With the Lord's help, he had done his job well, like a soldier who has completed his mission or a runner who has finished a race.

Are you living so that in the end you will have no regrets? Endeavor, by God's grace, to live each day to its fullest, and to give your all.

> *Lord, the race is long, but I am committed to running well as You fill me with strength. Empower me to live this very day in such a way that I will finish it with no regrets. Amen.*

The
Hidden You

The vast majority of an iceberg is hidden underwater. And what's true about icebergs is true about you. Your inner life, much like the mass of an iceberg, is hidden from the public eye. Yet the way you handle your secret life will have an impact on the part that people can see.

Which is why the Bible says, "Be sure your sin will find you out" (Numbers 32:23). And, "As [a man] thinks in his heart, so is he" (Proverbs 23:7). Whatever is true about your heart will eventually surface for all to see.

Only when your inner life is right will your outer life be right as well. Is there anything you need to bring to God today so the hidden part of you doesn't impair your outer influence?

> *Father, You are the only one who knows everything in my heart. Cleanse me, Lord, and heal me so that I can live with a whole heart and a pure and single focus. Amen.*

Cultivating Inner Purity

What are some practical ways you can keep your inner life pure?

- Develop firm convictions about doing what is right according to God's Word.
- Maintain a life of discipline that encourages holiness and avoids temptation.
- Make sure your goals are God-centered and not self-centered.
- Hide God's Word in your heart so it shapes your decisions and choices.
- Live a servant-oriented life focused on others rather than self.

Yielding your inner life to God in these ways will empower you to live the kind of outer life that honors the Lord and blesses others.

God, I want to live my life from the inside out today. May my convictions, personal discipline, and goals be up-to-date and shaped by Your Word. Help me to serve others with a pure heart. Amen.

Committing to Excellence

Legendary football coach Vince Lombardi said, "The quality of your life will be determined by the depth of your commitment to excellence, no matter what your chosen field." With that in mind, here are some questions you can ask yourself:

- What are the most important commitments in my life?
- Can I honestly say I'm giving my best to those commitments?
- How can I do better at carrying out those commitments, and what price am I willing to pay to make that happen?

Those questions will help you evaluate your priorities, and your answers will enable you to determine how to best spend your time and energy.

Lord, help me to be honest today as I assess what I'm actually committed to. Do I need to reprioritize my commitments? What steps do I need to take to follow through? Lead me, Lord. Amen.

Going Beyond
What Is Expected

To excel at something is to go over and above the normal. It means doing more than what is expected. It's about taking the extra step, the extra time, the extra effort in whatever you do. Yes, it's hard work, but in the end, if you persevere, it'll pay off.

Taking extra time with your wife and children will result in closer, stronger relationships with them. Going the extra mile on the job will gain appreciation from your boss and co-workers. Giving that extra effort as you serve in your church or help someone in need will bring blessing to others.

Without question, it pays to give your very best. Won't you ask the Lord to strengthen your resolve to strive for excellence in all that you do?

Father, show me today where I have been cutting corners. Empower me through Your Word and Spirit to go beyond what is expected and to demonstrate Your amazing love. Amen.

Imparting Your Life

One reason the apostle Paul's ministry still affects us today is that he was thoroughly focused on pouring his life into other people. To the church leaders in Ephesus he said, "I kept back nothing that was helpful" (Acts 20:20), and he did this for three years (verse 31). To the Christians in Thessalonica he said, "We were well pleased to impart to you...our own lives" (1 Thessalonians 2:8). And he worked with Timothy for 15 years, equipping him to carry the baton of leadership.

The famous preacher John Wesley said, "God buries his workmen, but His work goes on." Are you that kind of workman? Are you pouring yourself into others, including your children? If so, your impact will continue long after you're gone.

> God, help me to honestly assess my impact on others. Whom should I pour my life into? How should I do that? May I influence others for good through the power of Your Spirit. Amen.

A Pattern
to Follow

Jesus was the greatest mentor of all time. He took a ragtag group of uneducated, ill-equipped men and, in three years, molded them into a force that turned the world upside down. Here's what we can learn from His example:

There can be no impact without contact. Jesus spent time with His men. He taught by word and example, cared for them, and was patient with them.

He looked for men who were willing to learn. When He called them to the ministry, they eagerly followed. They made mistakes, but were willing to listen and obey.

He expected His disciples to make disciples. Jesus commanded them to carry on His work. We're now a part of that work, and we're to pass it on to others.

> *Lord, empower me today to follow Your example. Help me to pay attention to others, to learn from them, and to offer my input when they are willing to receive it. Amen.*

Assessing Your Impact

The closer you get to another person, the more influence you will have on that person's life.

And that brings up some important questions: Who are you getting close to? Who are you pouring your life into? Will you one day be able to join the apostle Paul in saying, "I have fought the good fight, I have finished the race" (2 Timothy 4:7) because you have equipped others to excel in following the Lord and serving Him?

Remember that it's not numbers or stature that's important here. Influencing your children and those closest to you takes priority over those outside your home. And it's far better to influence a few people well than many people poorly. Adhering to these principles will help you to finish the race well.

Father, does my family feel close to me? Whom am I influencing for good? Help me to be a good steward of the relationships You have given me. Amen.

Your Legacy

What will you leave behind when you are gone? As you well know, only that which is spiritual will last. If all you leave behind are personal memories, they will fade with time. If you leave financial security and provisions, that will take care of people's temporary physical needs, but nothing more.

By contrast, if you leave a godly example and you've helped people grow more spiritually strong, you'll have given gifts that last for eternity. You'll have left treasures that can be passed on to future generations of believers. That, in a very real way, is what it means to "lay up for yourselves treasures in heaven" rather than on earth (Matthew 6:19-20).

God, how is my heavenly treasure account doing? Show me today some simple ways that I can make a lasting impression on others and help them follow You. Amen.

Men
Growing Men

You are most likely very grateful for those spiritually mature men who have taken the time to help you grow as a Christian. Likewise, everything you do for the next generation of Christian men will elicit their gratitude as well.

When it comes to choosing the right men to pour your life into, what should you look for?

- Look for *faithful* men. Find men who are trustworthy, who keep their word.
- Look for *available* men. Find men who are willing to sacrifice their time for ministry training.
- Look for *teachable* men. Find men who are eager to learn. Their hunger will ensure your time and energy are well-spent.

Lord, the thought of pouring my life into younger Christians is a bit intimidating. Open the doors, I pray, and help me to simply share with others the things You have taught me. Amen.

A Living Bible

Have you ever considered that for some people in your life, you might be the only Christian they know? They may see believers on TV or in the newspaper, but often those portrayals are in a negative light. You may be the only one they can interact with in person. It's been said in a poem that "you are a living Bible, known and read by men." The rhyme goes on to ask, "What does the Bible say, 'according to you'?"

So are you exhibiting a proper representation of Christianity? Are you kind, thoughtful, and approachable? What would people say about God based on what they see of your life? What does the Bible say, according to you?

Father, this sounds like such a responsibility! Are You sure You want me to be Your representative? But I'm willing, Lord—please speak to others through my words and actions. Amen.

Well Done!

There is coming a day when your time on earth will end. But hopefully that won't be true about your influence as a man after God's own heart. No, as you are faithful to pour your life into your family, your friends, your workmates, and fellow believers at church, your influence will live on in their lives. You'll be gone, but God's work done through you will continue. You, as His messenger, will no longer speak, but God's message will live on.

May you never lose sight of the calling to live as a man after God's own heart. For in the end, you'll get the greatest reward anyone could ever hope to receive—that of hearing the Lord Jesus Christ say to you, "Well done, good and faithful servant."

God, I don't know how many decades I will have to serve You, but I do know I have today. When this very day ends, may I sense You whispering, "Well done." Amen.

More Insights for Men
Who Make a Difference

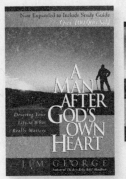

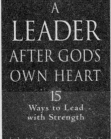

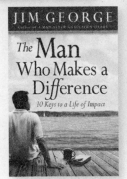

About the Author...

Jim George and his wife, Elizabeth, are bestselling authors and national speakers dedicated to helping people live a life after God's own heart. Together, they have written over 70 books with more than 8 million copies sold. For over 30 years, the teachings and steadfast example of Jim and Elizabeth have helped countless men and women.

Jim is a two-time finalist for the Gold Medallion Book Award. Besides writing, he has served as a pastor, seminary professor, and as a pharmacist with the Medical Service Corps of the Army Reserve. Jim's leadership influence has helped thousands of men honor God by modeling integrity in the workplace, learn to be better communicators, and build a strong legacy for their family. Jim holds a Bachelor of Science in Pharmacy from the University of Oklahoma and a Master of Divinity and Master of Theology from Talbot School of Theology.

www.elizabethgeorge.com
Facebook: www.facebook.com/ElizabethJimGeorge
Twitter: @jimupdates